MARGED
Strong Woman of Snowdonia

First published: 2010

ISBN: 978-1-84527-268-5

Cover design: Design Department of the Welsh Books Council

Published with the financial support of the
Welsh Books Council

Published by
Gwasg Carreg Gwalch, 12 Iard yr Orsaf, Llanrwst, Wales LL26 0EH
01492 642031 01492 641502
llyfrau@carreg-gwalch.com
Internet: www.carreg-gwalch.com

Welsh Women

2

Marged

Strong Woman of Snowdonia

Siân Lewis

Illustrated by Giles Greenfield

Big Jack wasn't just hungry. He was starving. He'd done a hard day's work at Llanberis copper mine, and now he was looking forward to his supper.

Jack had left a juicy joint of ham simmering on the hearth. As soon as he reached home, he removed the meat from the pot. He cut a tiny slice and stuffed it in his mouth. Then he left the rest to drain on a plate, while he went down to the lake to wash the dust from his hair and beard.

As he walked back to his cottage in the warm evening breeze, Jack rubbed his large stomach contentedly. The smell of the ham wafted towards him.

Mmmm!

What a smell! It was so delicious that he stopped on the doorstep and breathed in deeply to enjoy it all the more.

In the middle of breathing in, Jack choked. His eyes popped. Was he dreaming? Was he having a horrible nightmare? His plate was still sitting squarely in the middle of the table, but where was the meat? Apart from a trickle of juice, his supper had gone.

Jack stumbled over the doorstep. 'Where's my meat?' he croaked. He snatched up the empty plate. 'Where's my meat?' he wailed.

A drop of gleaming juice ran over his fingers and dripped onto the earth floor. As Jack sucked his fingers, he saw more drops, a long trail of them leading out through the door.

'Someone has stolen my meat!' hissed Jack. 'I'll get him, whoever he is.' He dropped the plate and, with rage boiling up in his heart, out through the door he ran, and down the side path.

The trail of drops disappeared into the vegetable patch at the back of the cottage.

In that vegetable patch Jack heard a noise.

A happy chewing noise.

In the middle of the turnip row he saw a tail.

A happy wagging tail.

Out of the turnip leaves popped a terrier's head. Hanging from its mouth was a lump of ham.

'ARRRRRRRGH!' Jack's roar of rage was the last thing the terrier heard. Two rough hands closed around his throat and, moments later, the dog's limp body went flying through the air. It dropped with a splash into the waters of Padarn lake.

'Serve you right, you scoundrel!' roared Jack, dusting his hands. Jack was a bad-tempered man, who liked to throw his weight around. The one thing he enjoyed more than food was revenge. So with an ugly smile on his face he made his way back to his cottage.

But Jack wouldn't have been smiling if he'd known who was heading towards him at that very moment. The owner of the dead terrier was a fearsome lady called Marged, daughter of Ifan. Marged was out looking for her pet, and drawing ever closer to Jack's home.

No wonder people were scared of Marged, daughter of Ifan. She was an immensely tall, strong woman with jet black hair and hands like shovels. One of her hobbies was wrestling, and she was such an excellent wrestler, that she could beat men less than half her age.

Marged was born on a farm in the Nantlle Valley in

1696, and as she grew older, she became so famous that people travelled for miles in the hope of seeing her. One of those travellers was the writer, Thomas Pennant.

When Thomas Pennant first heard of Marged, she was the innkeeper at Y Telyrniau in her home village. Y Telyrniau was probably the quietest inn in the whole of Wales. Though many of the drinkers were tough, hardworking men from the nearby Drws-y-coed copper mine, they became gentle as lambs as soon as they set foot inside. They knew that if there was any rowdy behaviour, Marged would throw them out.

'Don't you dare set foot in here till you learn how to behave,' she would bellow, as she bundled them over the doorstep, sometimes as many as six at a time.

Her voice, echoing around the hilltops, was enough to send shivers down men's backs. No one shivered more than her husband, a thin little mouse of a man whose name was Richard Morris. Marged gave Richard two good hidings, so it's said. After the first hiding, he promised to marry her. After the second, he gave up drinking.

Thomas Pennant was very impressed by Marged. In spirit and strength she reminded him of the warrior-women of the ancient Britons. But other people were not quite so complimentary. They wrote poems that made fun of Marged. Though they called her 'gentle Marged', their poems proved that she wasn't gentle at all.

Gentle Marged, daughter of Ifan,
Has a large clog and a small one:
One to stir a stubborn hound,
The other to kick her husband around.

Gentle Margaret, daughter of Ifan,
Has a large hook and a small one:
One to drag the hounds from bed,
The other to break a person's head.

If these verses are true, Marged wasn't a person to be admired. Yet, we still remember her today, and her name appears in dictionaries of biography, alongside other famous people.

The reason we remember her is because there was another side to Marged. Yes, she was big and strong, and maybe a bully at times, but she was also a woman who made use of her size and stamina in extraordinary ways.

In Marged's time there weren't any shops as we know them today. Instead, in every locality, there were skilled craftsmen.

If you wanted a pair of shoes, you went to the shoemaker.

If you wanted cloth, you went to a weaver.

If you wanted a table or chair, you went to the carpenter.

But what did Marged do?

If Marged wanted a pair of sturdy shoes for her enormous feet, she cut, hammered and stitched, and made them herself.

If she wanted cloth, she sheared the sheep, spun the wool, and wove the cloth.

If she wanted her horse shod, she didn't go to a blacksmith. She was strong and determined enough to do the work herself.

And if she wanted a harp made, did she go to the carpenter or the harpmaker? Of course not. She made her own harp.

You may be wondering what a big bellowing woman like Marged would want with a harp. In fact Marged could sing very sweetly and, though her fingers were large, they moved very nimbly across the harpstrings. She could play the violin too. (Guess who made it?) She was a talented musician, who could play any number of folk-songs. She also composed her own songs, both words and music. The folk-song Merch Megan may well have been written by Marged.

On sunny days Marged would step outside Y Telyrniau and play her harp or violin while her customers danced. Her husband Richard was also a harpist, and according to this verse, he even enjoyed his wife's music.

Gentle Marged, daughter of Ifan,
Has a large harp and a small one;
One to play in Caernarfon town
And one to smooth her husband's frown.

Despite Marged's talents Y Telyrniau fell on hard times. For a while the mine at Drws-y-coed stopped working, and the

Y
TELYRNIAU

miners had to go elsewhere to earn their living. Marged and Richard packed their bags too. They moved a few miles north to the foot of Snowdon, and settled in Pen Llyn, close to the little village of Cwm-y-glo near Llanberis.

Pen Llyn means 'the end of the lake'. Marged's home stood near the shores of Lake Padarn, and it was on the waters of that lake, and on nearby Lake Peris, that she found work. A woman as strong and determined as Marged could not remain idle for long. Instead of keeping a pub, she became a boatwoman for the Llanberis copper mine. Because the roads were so poor, the only way of shifting the ore from the mine was to load it onto ponies, who carried it down the mountain to the shores of Lake Peris. There boats would ferry it across the lakes.

A boatwoman needs a boat, so how did Marged get hold of hers? Did she visit a local boatbuilder? Of course not. Marged made her own. Why make work for others when you can do it yourself? A boat such as Marged used was rescued from the waters of Lake Padarn some years ago, and is now in the Llanberis Slate Museum.

Marged became known as 'The Queen of the Lakes'. Back and forth she would row with her loads of ore. The rowing kept her muscles in trim, which was one reason why she was such a good wrestler. It was back-breaking work, and Marged's only helper was her maid, who was almost as strong as herself. Her maid worked alongside Marged for forty years, till her death in 1786.

Sometimes Marged took passengers in her boat. On one occasion she took a local gentleman called Mr Smith. 'Ha!' thought Mr Smith to himself. 'This'll be a good story to tell my friends. I'll tell them I went out on the lake with a giantess. I'll even tell them I stole a kiss.'

As Marged rowed far from shore, Mr Smith sat in the front of the boat grinning cheekily. He waited till Marged had reached the middle of the lake, then leaned forward, puckered up his lips and...

SLAP!

Mr Smith's lips never got anywhere near Marged's cheek. Instead a large hand picked him up by the scruff of the neck. Moments later there was a resounding SPLASH, as Mr Smith landed in the cold waters of Lake Padarn.

The poor man couldn't swim.

'Help! Help!' he wailed, as he clawed at the side of the boat. 'Save me! Save me!'

'I'll save you, if you give me a guinea,' sniffed Marged.

'Yes, yes! I promise!' wailed Mr Smith.

A hand gripped him once more by the scruff of the neck and hauled him into the boat.

Mr Smith, after paying his debt, skulked home. He never told his friends the story, but they all got to hear of it. There had been plenty of watchers on the lakeside, who had enjoyed the show.

There was one other passenger, a far better-behaved passenger, whom Marged liked to take with her in her boat. This was her little terrier, Ianto. Marged was a keen huntress. On the chimneybreast of her cottage there were a hundred and ninety marks, one for each fox she had caught. To hunt the foxes she kept a pack of dogs. She kept spaniels and terriers and greyhounds, all with gleaming coats. But of all her many dogs, her favourite was Ianto.

Ianto was generally an obedient dog, but one day, while Marged was unloading the copper ore at the jetty, he decided to go for a walk in the woods. Those woods were full of exciting smells that turned Ianto's head. He ran this way and that. He chased birds and leaves. He barked at scurrying mice. Farther and farther into the woods he went, sniffing around rabbit holes and poking his head into badgers' setts. He was having such fun, he didn't notice he was lost till the sun began to set. Then he looked round and barked sharply.

No-one heard him.

He sat on the ground, lifted his nose and howled.

Still no one heard him.

In the far distance, on the shores of the lake, Marged was asking everyone, 'Where's Ianto? Have you seen Ianto?'

'Well, I did see a little terrier wander off into the woods,' said a woman. 'It was ages ago, mind.'

'Ianto! Ianto!' Marged shouted, but loud though her voice was, Ianto was too far away to hear.

Into the woods went Marged, still calling and calling.

In the meantime Ianto's stomach was rumbling. If he'd been at home, Marged would have fed him by now. The little dog scratched behind his ear. What do you do if no one feeds you? You have to find food for yourself. That's what Marged would have done.

So Ianto got up and went in search of food. He sniffed rabbits, but they were too fast for him. He sniffed birds, but they flew out of his way. Then he sniffed again. This time he smelled a most delicious smell, the sort of smell he'd smelled in Marged's kitchen. Whenever Marged cooked a joint of meat, she would throw the bone to him, and he would suck it and gnaw it till every drop of juice had gone.

Ianto picked up speed. Soon he was bounding along in the direction of that smell. He burst through the trees and there in front of him was a cottage with its door open wide. He ran up the path and skidded over the doorstep.

He barked excitedly.

On the table was a plate, and on that plate was a glistening, dripping joint of meat. Ianto barked again. No one answered. No one shouted, 'Don't you dare touch that meat, boy!' So Ianto jumped up on a chair, helped himself to the meat and ran out of the cottage. He knew his manners. He knew he wasn't allowed to eat inside a house, so off he scampered into the back garden.

The joint of meat was so big, it dropped from his mouth and rolled along the path. He ran after it, then dragged in across to a shady spot in a turnip row. There he sank his teeth into it, and made happy chewing noises.

He was chewing so noisily he didn't hear the footsteps on the front path. He didn't hear the clatter of a plate in the kitchen. He did hear a sort of rumble coming towards him, but that didn't stop him eating. He was still chewing when a large man hurtled round the corner of the house.

He went on chewing till the man's hands closed around his neck. Moments later, as his limp body dropped into Lake Padarn, a last mouthful of meat dropped from his jaws and spread like a starfish on the water.

Meanwhile Marged was still looking for him.

'Ianto! Ianto bach! Ianto, where are you? Come to Marged!' she called, as she made her way through the

woods in the direction of Jack's cottage.

She was walking along the shores of the lake, when she saw a sight that made her blood run cold. Bobbing along in the ripples at the water's edge was a small body.

'Ianto!' wailed Marged, wading into the water and scooping him up. His head flopped against her arm, and she saw that his neck was broken. She looked around. Jack was watching from the door of his cottage.

'Is that scoundrel yours?' he growled at her.

'Scoundrel?' Marged laid Ianto on a rock and waded out of the water. 'Who are you calling a scoundrel?' she asked.

'That dog of yours,' snapped Jack. 'He ate my joint of meat.'

'And you killed him for that?' hissed Marged, striding up to him. 'I would have paid for that meat. I would have paid for it four times over.'

'So you say!' sneered Jack.

'I would!' insisted Marged. 'I'm a fair woman. I know my dog did wrong, but he didn't deserve to die for it. He was hungry and he was lost.'

'Well, he's definitely lost now.' Jack laughed and spat in the direction of Ianto's body.

Marged clenched her fists hard. She was not going to lose her temper. Not yet.

'I'll still give you the money for the meat,' she said. 'But you've got to pay for my dog.'

'Who says?' said Big Jack. He wasn't scared of Marged.

They were almost the same size. In fact when he stood on his doorstep, he was taller than she was, and could look down his nose at her.

'I do,' said Marged.

'And why should I do what you say?' sneered Jack, turning his back on her. 'Push off!' he called over his shoulder.

It only took a second for Marged to grab hold of the miner's shoulder and spin him round. The last thing Jack saw before he fell to the floor was the sight of a large fist coming towards him. While he was still moaning and groaning, Marged stepped over him. In the cottage she found enough money to pay for her dog.

'Right! That's settled,' she said, and stopping only to bury little Ianto in the woods, she set off home leaving Jack to nurse his sore jaw.

If Jack had been wise, he wouldn't have stood up to Marged. Most men would have known better. It was said that Marged had helped to lay the slate bridge at Pont Meibion, Nant Peris. She'd lifted up one end of the huge slate slab on her own, while a gang of young men struggled to lift up the other end. Who could tackle a woman like that?

Marged was so strong and healthy, she was still wrestling at the age of seventy. She lived a very long life. According to the poem on her gravestone in Nant Peris, she was 92 when she died, but she may well have been much older. Some say that she lived from 1696 to 1801, which would have made her 105 years old.

In the poem she is called 'Peggy Evans'. 'Peggy' is a pet name for 'Marged' and 'Evans' means 'child of Ifan.'

Here lies Peggy Evans who saw ninety two,
Could wrestle, row, fiddle, and hunt a fox too,
Could ring a sweet peal, as the neighbourhood tells,
That would cheer your two ears – had there been any bells.
Enjoyed rosy health in a lodging of straw,
Commanded the saw pit, and wielded the saw.
And though she's departed where you cannot find her,
I know she has left a few sisters behind her.

If the poem is true, there must have been other women as strong as Marged, but none were so clever, none so determined, and none so talented in so many different ways.

If you had to write a poem about Marged, how would you describe her?

* The 'Gentle Marged' poems are adapted from the Welsh.

Tales from Wales 1

Fairy Tales from Wales

There are many stories about the 'little people' of Wales – here are four of them.

Tales from Wales 2

King Arthur's Cave

Imagine the surprise of a young shepherd who discovers a cave full of treasure and sleeping soldiers . . .

Tales from Wales 3

The Faithful Dog, Gelert

A starving wolf in a baby's room, and Gelert – Prince Llywelyn's favourite hunting hound – has to fight for his life . . .